Grain

John Glenday was born in Broughty Ferry in 1952. His first collection, *The Apple Ghost*, won a Scottish Arts Council Book Award and his second, *Undark*, was a Poetry Book Society Recommendation, as was his third, *Grain*. He lives in Cawdor, and works for NHS Highland as an addictions counsellor.

Also by John Glenday

The Apple Ghost
Undark

Grain

John Glenday

PICADOR

First published 2009 by Picador
an imprint of Pan Macmillan, a division of Macmillan Publishers Limited
Pan Macmillan, 20 New Wharf Road, London N1 9RR
Basingstoke and Oxford
Associated companies throughout the world
www.panmacmillan.com

ISBN 978-0-330-46134-4

9 8 7 6 5 4 3 2

A CIP catalogue record for this book is available
from the British Library.

Printed and bound in the UK by
CPI Group (UK) Ltd, Croydon, CR0 4YY

Acknowledgements

Poems or earlier versions, have appeared in the following publications and periodicals:

100 Favourite Scottish Love Poems; *100 Favourite Scottish Poems*; *Carapace 18*; *Chapman*; *Comparative Criticism 19*; *Inspired? Get Writing!*; *London Review of Books*; *Love for Love*; *New British Poetry*; *Northwords Now*; *Poetry (Chicago)*; *Poetry Ireland Review*; *Riptide*; *Skein of Geese*; *Such Strange Joy*.

'Calm Water at Mill Bay' appeared in *There's a Poem to be Made* – in celebration of Stewart Conn's seventieth birthday (Shore Poets, 2006).

'Genesis' was first published in poster form at the Salisbury Last Words Festival and subsequently appeared in the anthology *Last Words* (Picador, 2000).

'Imagine You are Driving' won the 2006/7 National Galleries of Scotland Creative Writing Competition.

'Yesnaby' was first broadcast on BBC Radio Scotland in 2004.

The writer gratefully acknowledges support from the Scottish Arts Council towards the writing of this title.

My grateful thanks to all those who provided encouragement, comments, accommodation, and dogged support, but especially Joyce Caplan, Bill Duncan, Andrew Greig and Gail Wylie, and to Kathleen Jamie and Don Paterson for their careful reading and suggestions for the manuscript.

Contents

Grain

Epitaph

Father, forgive this man.
He never listened to your song
till it was all but done
then found he couldn't sing the words
so he spoke the tune.

Imagine You are Driving

Imagine you are driving
nowhere, with no one beside you;
with the empty road unravelling and ravelling
in sympathy as the wheel turns in your hands.

On either side the wheatfields go shimmering
past in an absence of birdsong, and the sky
decants the shadows of the weather from itself.
So you drive on, hopeful of a time

when the ocean will rise up before you like dusk
and you will make landfall at last –
some ancient, long-forgotten mooring,
which both of you, of course, will recognise;

though as I said before, there is no one beside you
and neither of you has anywhere to go.

The River

This is my formula for the fall of things:
we come to a river we always knew we'd have to cross.
It ferries the twilight down through fieldworks

of corn and half-blown sunflowers.
The only sounds, one lost cicada calling to itself
and the piping of a bird that will never have a name.

Now tell me there is a pause
where we know there should be an end;
then tell me you too imagined it this way

with our shadows never quite touching the river
and the river never quite reaching the sea.

At Innernytie

for Gail and Sandy Wylie

All we can ever hear
is the slipping by of things
as another night comes down.

Everything changes forever;
everything remains.
The elderflower moon

the rapefield's cadmium
and the lark's voice,
widening into silence like a river.

Listen:
beyond the heart's breath
and the lingering soul,

beyond the last bee
dying in the honeysuckle,
beyond the cirrus and the fallstreaks

of tomorrow's rain –
the sound of things becoming
what they never will again.

Landscape with Flying Man

I read about him that was given wings.
His father fixed those wings to carry him away.

They carried him halfway home, and then he fell.
And he fell not because he flew

but because he loved it so. You see
it's neither pride, nor gravity but love

that pulls us back down to the world.
Love furnishes the wings, and that same love

will watch over us as we drown.
The soul makes a thousand crossings, the heart, just one.

Etching of a Line of Trees

i.m. John Goodfellow Glenday

I carved out the careful absence of a hill and a hill grew.
I cut away the fabric of the trees
and the trees stood shivering in the darkness.

When I had burned off the last syllables of wind,
a fresh wind rose and lingered.
But because I could not bring myself

to remove you from that hill,
you are no longer there. How wonderful it is
that neither of us managed to survive

when it was love that surely pulled the burr
and love that gnawed its own shape from the burnished air
and love that shaped that absent wind against a tree.

Some shadow's hands moved with my hands
and everything I touched was turned to darkness
and everything I could not touch was light.

What My Mother Called Me

The human heart, I am led to believe, is the same size as a clenched fist. And so it was that in that single heartbeat between the last beam of last night's dark and the deep, grey first light of today I caught sight of who else but, coincidence itself, my mother settling from the air. She was built from the old smoke stacked in a shuttered room. Light in the air as the last of hopefulness, she batted the dandelion clocks of her fists towards the draught, pulled herself clear of the peeling bedroom wall, one hand to the place her heart had been. And in the moment between forming and her own words dissolving her again and me thinking all that about the human heart; its size, her hands, that room, and the messy rest, she mouthed the word it was she had called me by, which was my father's also, with an upturn to its only syllable, as if it were a question she had never framed before.

St Orage

Preserve us, St Orage, you whose image stares down
on our weed-snagged railway sidings and choked
factory yards; whose relics crumble in a cardboard box
in a hampered lock-up somewhere. We await your word.

St Eadfast and St Alwart, we rely on you
to indicate the Good Path, however stony.
Lead us not into that rock-strewn gully
clogged with St Randed's bones.

Oh Lord, we know your faithful
knew more deaths than we had fingers –
St Ifle and St Rangle and St Arving and St Ab, all
flew into your mercy through their disparate anguishes.

But most of all, remember us yourselves,
forgotten saints we here commemorate:
St Agger of the drunken brawling praise;
St Ainless, martyred on the lopped branch of his perfect life;

St Anza, stunned by her own reverberating song;
and blameless, maculate St Igmata, dead and forgiving child,
who even in the crib, they say, held up her little punctured hands
in wonder and in ignorance, and cried.

A Fairy Tale

She had been living happily ever before,
waltzing through imagined ballrooms in the arms
of a handsome young prince. Then, one day, they kiss
for the first time, he takes back the word love

and suddenly bloats to an idle, wounded beast
that stoops above her in its thickening hide.
She trembles before his laboured breath and white, strange eyes.
Each night from her solitary bed, she overhears the echoes

of unimaginable rages which transform their castle
to a ruin of shadowy rooms with a cursed and sleeping heart.
At last she understands him poorly enough to be terrified
and run a gauntlet of scattering wolves to the arms of her sick father

who greets her with a tearful goodbye. They subsist
forever after on a diet of simple gruel and vague desire.
When passers-by ask her about her life, she waltzes the laundry
to her heart and answers with a distant smile: *Once upon a time.*

The Man Rats Loved

That wasn't much of a tune you played:
just a few sour notes fingered for your own pleasure

as you pranced through my childhood
(such a meagre town) half dressed as the mother,

half as the father and neither half fitting right.
I didn't fall for you, but followed anyway, eager

enough to trust my luck wherever you might lead,
under the hill or into the swollen river.

Valentine

suck my red heart white, I will, because I love you, bless me,
o, and here, I will say, see I am back, in spite of you to bring
a gift I grew, it was busy in me once, filled the red branches
with blood, knocking like hope, beat time to my life's decline,
then followed after in its way, and did its duty.

Lub Dup

"The characteristic sounds of a normal heartbeat as heard in auscultation" *(Merriam-Webster's Medical Dictionary)*

Why is it always the lame boy
who volunteers the only path
who hobbles along beside us
promising he'll never rest
till he has shown us
where the buried children are
and we have laid ourselves
on the lee slope of the hill
that closed itself against him,
heady with muffled
flutesong; distant laughter?

The Afterlife

Because I could I did – build her I mean – from bits I found,
the scraps of being no one else would have – harvested
organs, glands that set the balance, patchwork features still
the shape of who they were before they weren't, all hooked
to a sack of blood and made to go somewhat. Bones hinged in
their proper order, muscles flinched, the milk set in her eyes
(a close match, not a pair). Somehow it worked. A marvel.
God knows how. You should have seen me gaff the weather
at its worst, all broken lights and wattage, then earth the
brilliance through her. Took this for a show of love though
she kicked with a reek of burn. It straddled every sinew,
grounded at last in her opening face. One lid went back, she
gazed up through my downward gaze, through the scaffolding
of lights and instruments, on into overarching mirk. Then
just as the current died the grey rag of her lips tore open for
a moment and the air, forced through her throat's reed, broke
with a play of notes, almost like song.

The Kelp Eaters

Hydrodamalis gigas

These beasts are four fathoms long, but perfectly gentle.
They roam the shallower waters like sea-cattle

and graze on the waving flags of kelp.
At the slightest wound their innards will flop

out with a great hissing sound,
but they have not yet grown to fear mankind:

no matter how many of their number might be killed,
they never try to swim away, they are so mild.

When one is speared, its neighbours will rush in
and struggle to draw out the harpoon

with the blades of their little hooves.
They almost seem to have a grasp of what it is to love.

I once watched a bull return to its butchered
mate two days in a row, butting its flensed hide

and calling out quietly across the shingle till the darkness fell.
The flesh on the small calves tastes as sweet as veal

and their fat is pleasantly coloured,
like the best Dutch butter.

The females are furnished with long, black teats.
When brushed hard with a fingertip

even on the dead
they will grow firm and the sweet milk bleed.

from 'Journal of a Voyage with Bering 1741–1742'
by Georg Wilhelm Steller

The Ugly

I love you as I love the Hatchetfish,
the Allmouth, the Angler,
the Sawbelly and Wolf-eel,
the Stoplight Loosejaw, the Fangtooth;

all our sweet bathypelagic ones,
and especially those too terrible or sly
even for Latin names; who staple
their menfolk to the vagina's hide

like scorched purses, stiff with seed;
whom God built to trawl
endless cathedrals of darkness,
their bland eyes gaping like sores;

who would choke down hunger itself,
had it pith and gristle enough;
who carry on their foreheads
the trembling light of the world.

And What is It?

And what is it?

Listen and I will tell you. It is an animal. It belongs to a phylum. It came from an ancient sea, an egg; it swung through the pitch of a mother's womb. Once upon a time it breathed with gills. It is a bitch that will become a dog, a hen changed into a cock; it is the little girl who grows up to be a boy; a princess who would be king. It procreates and becomes as a multitude. It seeks the warmth of the herd yet desires to be alone.

What is this thing made from?

Yes, I know what it is made from. It has been made from salt, cartilage, epithelium, fur, enzymes, water, bone; its eyes face one way, towards its food. It has teeth for tearing and jaws for mastication. Each limb is decked in vestigial claws. If you ask me who made it I will tell you God made it.

What is it called?

Well I can tell you its name. This is its name: it has a common name and a Latin binomial. It has an official name and it has been granted an individual name. Perhaps it turns its head when this name is enunciated. And it has a secret name for itself that it mouths without breath at times of a certain nature.

But what does it do?

What it does is this: it walks upright, but it may crawl on four legs, or hang by its limbs. It flies on fins that trawl the air; it pulls itself towards sunlight, scuttles towards stones. It takes itself a mate – occasionally for life, but more often for a shorter period of time. It smells of itself. It can briefly gallop. It burrows and ascends. It swims when there is a need for swimming. It lifts an opposing thumb and touches this thumb against a fingertip. It does this again. It is both known and unknown.

Does this animal make a sound?
Yes. It makes for itself the sounds of many calls. I have often heard them. It calls out even towards the emptiness. Listen now: it grunts; it whimpers, it whines; it snarls. It sings and all the other species listen.

Where is it now?
Here it is that has stumbled in through a door of an empty house. Whose home is this house, I ask? No. I do not know. I do not know this house. This animal is stationed before a window of the house. The window contains an interesting prospect: such a great shelving perspective of similar houses and their shadows and a falling of rain.

What is it doing now?
Come with me and we shall see what this animal is doing. Come along with me now and we shall see.

Glen Dye

by that flinch in the Water of Dye
where its wersh soul swithers
through the Bog of Luchray
and on towards the Dee,
there runs a certain gentleness
of ragged stonework in an old sheep fank,
where a flush of broom pushes out;
and if you happened to lie in its doubtful lee,
come early spring, you might just hear
the wind go clambering through, fluting
a note or two from a threadbare melody,
for nothing but its own sake.

For Lucie

born 5 December 2005

How apt it was we named you
for the light: no more than a small light, mind

– a spunk; a spill; a stub of tallow
cradled against the draft

while our stooped shadows lengthen
and fall away behind.

Here's to you, then, and to us,
to your world and to ours.

We raise you towards the dark.
May you make of it something else.

Genesis

The United Materialist Church believe
that at any given moment God demolishes the world,
only to rebuild it instantly, altered and oblivious.

Everything from our first formlessness
to the final blare of light testifies
to this infinite substantiation of His love.

Their Bible consists of just the one book,
predictably named Genesis.
Here we may read of that strange bush consumed

in a terrible caul of silence; and the lost garden,
without fruit and without serpent,
where the hopeful naked wait with the hopeful innocent.

Sermon

On all sides his absence arranges itself. Can you feel him move? He is so small and everywhere, like blown ash or cotton frets. He flutters in the closed hand. His name a tiny breath in a breath. He is all things, inside all things, seeking himself. His body so light it winnows itself; chaff in the wind. He is the midge that sings for your blood that you may be one with him. Look at this room, this world, it is so small, the darkness streaming from the windows; and he smaller than anything, a fleck of desire. Can you feel it, the small ballast of your soul shifting? How inconsequential he is against the failing of the afternoon, riding with the dust to lightfall and shadow.

The Lily

Mair o a concept than a common flooer,
I daurdna pu the lily, that gaes
as the altar-cannle's metaphor.

An yet, as in the hert o a'thing pure,
Sae likewise wi the lily, whase
Sulphury yallow pollen bides its oor.

Promise

and the word lost for a single breath, as I lie against you; I promise everything that ever was will grow alive again: the first man in his sudden ignorance spits a sour apple whole, turns to her, who will be no more than an ache in the bones of his heart, as you are for me; for this breath, in my arms, the rain falling through the moment's light; then let me rest for one day, for the strength to unmake myself; the beasts of the earth and the great whales, to shift continents into oceans, to take down the firmament and blink into the failing light, the failing darkness for a moment's breath, a moment's touch, brushing your heart like this, as all things fall back into themselves, leaving nothing in the beginning but the word

The Garden

for Erika

Just for a quarter of a day, I'd have you
follow me through the smoking willow-herb
and my father's garden's half-seized gate,

down to that place where the knowledge
of almost everything comes undone
in the powdery ceanothus shade;

where the apple goes withering back to blossom
in your palm, and the serpent, on its hind legs
in the shadows, leaves off whispering.

Ark

Did we really believe
our love could have survived
on that boat something or other
had us build of spavined cedar
pitched and thatched against the flood,
with two of nothing but ourselves on board –
no raven to hoist behind the rain,
no dove returning with a sprig of green?

Tin

(the can opener was invented
forty-eight years after the tin can)

When you asked me for a love poem,
(*another* love poem) my thoughts
were immediately drawn to the early days

of the food canning industry –
all those strangely familiar trade-names from childhood:
Del Monte, Green Giant, Fray Bentos, Heinz.

I thought of Franklin and his poisoned men
drifting quietly northwest by north
towards the scooped shale of their graves

and I thought of the first tin of cling peaches
glowing on a dusty pantry shelf
like yet-to-be-discovered radium –

the very first tin of cling peaches
in the world, and for half a century
my fingers reaching out to it.

Mangurstadh

I send you the hush and founder
of the waves at Mangurstadh

in case there is too much
darkness in you now

and you need to remember
why it is we love

Exile

The heart, that other place, its people, ever since the war, whole continents adrift; rain falling, ash and dark; all borders distant or forgotten, all passports burned, all leave abruptly cancelled, all rumours true; and how small it is, you know, that place, and so little cared for: its children stolen, its people subjugate; and now so few, let me say, with everywhere strangers on the move; and yet despite it all, despite the hunger and the summary injustices, despite the stones I threw, still they came on, wherever I went, those ones remaining, hands lifted and empty, still they came after me and they asked – imagine this – they asked for you.

The Twins

for Sophie and Cameron Neville

How typical. Given your pick
of seven thousand stars, in all their
strange, familiar scaffoldings,

you had to choose the simplest:
two flecks of Knoydart mica, shivering
between Munlochy and the Firth.

How long ago and insulate
and frail they seemed – like God
and the shadow of his absence in our lives:

helplessly adrift between the dusk
and dark and dusk; but always together,
sailing together over everything.

Vitruvian Man

There was a time I tried picturing
the circumference of the soul
but the best I could manage

was a shimmery, milk-blue sun,
an oversized thought-bubble,
a zero with my height

which immediately reminded me
of that hoop he once transcribed
through a sweep of his sepia arms,

as he reached out beyond
the trammel of himself and caught hold
of nothing with both hands.

The Fist

Distance should give no cause for fret –
its threads can draw the lover and the loved
together, somehow – does that make sense?
Imagine, in the careful trammel of your fist,
firstly the flecked egg of a linnet, blessed
with a handsome clutch the rats would one day scoff –
remember, in that gorse bush by the old hayloft?
Secondly, the blown shell of an August moon,
rising above that field at Cantraywood
whose thread-worn light undressed our nakedness.
Now look into that hand again, and tell me this:
which of the aforesaid better fitted it?

Song

My hair:
four hundred leathery yards of sugar-wrack and tangle,
heaving beneath the cliff's club foot, on the west flank of
Connachair.

My brain:
a folded mattress with a bum-shaped stain, softening against
the far wall of a concrete drying green in Rutherglen.

My pineal body:
273c Baltic Street, Dundee.

My eyes:
two porcelain eggcups of seawater perched on the dashboard
of a soft-topped Lotus, half-way up (or down) the Bealach na
Ba, Applecross.

My tongue:
a threadbare stretch of tar macadam next to the last house
but one in Tongue.

My blood:
a stoppered length of old canal, blighted with drifts of
knotted condoms, buckled zimmer frames, several half-
burned Action Men and one small dog (bald, grinning,
dead) closed in a sunken novelty fridge. All this somewhere
between here and Linwood.

My hands:
splayed rhizomes of *Fallopia japonica*, clogging both banks
of a wee burn just beyond Prestonpans.

My breath:
a grey tide hefts and dims the foreshore weeds at Monifieth.

My heart:
that kicking, drowning thing in a weighted bag,
Sunday before last, when we pulled over for a comfort break
by Annan Water on the outskirts of Moffat.

My bum:
all of Oldmeldrum.

Blue

Blue: sweet colour of far away,
the colour of farewell,
the colour I remember

from your eyes.
A childhood blue once trembled
where the city stutters

into dusty scrub
and empty marshalling yards.
The last grim veil

of innocence was blue.
If I were asked to construct
a world that wasn't there

I'd make its every surface
scrupulously blue, and you
the only resident.

Stranger

Today, I am a new man,
a stranger in the town that bore me.

How simple it is to become a ghost –
just one word, one gesture, and we slip

through the fretwork of other people's lives
as easily as water through a stone.

Just for today, if I were to pass myself in the street
I wouldn't even raise my hat, or say hello.

The Uncertain

from the Hungarian

A white moth falls, dying,
like a torn scrap of paper,

or paper burned to ash,
or dogged summer snow,

or a petal from a mountain rose
discarded by a love-sick girl,

or a diploma of little worth
that holds not a single word

being the blank sum of all words in itself.
Look, poor thing, even as it passes away

it tries to read, opening and closing
the empty pages of its life.

Silence the Colour of Snow

Silence the colour of snow
settles against everything we love –
the late, startled flowers, the roadside stones –
all edges softened, all calamities blurred.

Why do you accuse me of never talking with you?
You know, they used to say that
if every tongue in the world were stilled at once,
the common silence would translate itself

to a snow that even our summer winds
could never drive away. Hush now, not another word.
Look! High over the frozen roofs,
my answer hangs and falls, that six-fingered star.

Remember those Wild Apples

Remember those wild apples
we would gather in the autumn, stained
with a half-faced blush, or the viridescent
shadow of a vanished leaf?
They clung to the early cold like a young girl's heart.

Grandfather said they were all seeded
from that first tree God espaliered in Paradise;
its fruit so bitter, even Adam felt compelled
to spread softened honey on the flesh
before he could savour exile, and the world.

A Westray Prayer

i.m. Mike and Barbara Heasman

Let us now give thanks
for these salt-blown

wind-burned pastures
where oatgrass and timothy
shrink from the harrow of the sea

where Scotland at long last
wearies of muttering its own name
where we may begin

to believe we have always known
what someone in his wisdom
must have meant

when he gave us everything
and told us nothing.

Calm Water at Mill Bay

for Stewart Conn

The moon is an empty dish
tipped over Hoy

its mackerel spill through
their own reflections

like petroleum.
The shadows that brought us here

are foundering on the foreshore
stones at Clett Skerry.

We drift in the pluck and lift
of something that is not the sea.

Grain

What was his name again – that fisher lad
dragged under with his fankled nets –
him that the fishes hooked and filleted?
I often wonder if the irony of it all amused him
as he left off from kicking against the dark, and drowned:
not, (as his Mother always feared) to be lost at sea, but found.

Tell me you've never seen a hangman hung,
nor laughed at the dying tenor, topped by his own song;
nor stumbled across a baker's corpse, rising like dough;
nor wept with the weeping ferryman while Charon
gummed his coin. Friends, we're all done for by the things we do.
If I were a farmer, I'd shrink from the ripening grain.

Loving Cup

You were the stone cup
brimmed with ash and shadow
I once prised from the coom
of a winter howe.

The dead sun drew
a smile of blood across my face,
spoke to me through
the shadow of my voice:

Man, it said, *this might be next to nothing*
and drawn through a bitter tap,
but it's all you'll ever have.
Don't spill a drop.

Island Song

I cannot see my mother's face;
no longer know my father's name.
It's the forgetting of the world
keeps me sane.

A stranger's laugh, a neighbour's death;
my wife's despair, my daughter's grief.
It's the forgetting of the world
gives me breath.

The hungry, old, surrounding sea,
heaves at a field's worn edge in me.
It's the forgetting of the world
sets us free.

Noust

Noust in the grass
grass in the wind
wind on the lark
lark for the sun

Sun through the sea
sea in the heart
heart in its noust
nothing is lost

Yesnaby

Not one of us will live forever –
the world is far too beautiful for that.

When my children ask about the War, I'll say:
'I once watched as columns of retreating cloud

burned in a haar of gulls and dust, off Yesnaby;
and I survived.'

Notes

Imagine You are Driving – after Julian Opie, 'Imagine You are Driving 1', 1997.

Etching of a Line of Trees is based on the etching 'Eye of the Wind' by Bill Duncan.

The Kelp Eaters draws heavily on G. W. Steller's *Journal of a Voyage with Bering, 1741–1742* translated by M. A. Engel and O. W. Frost (Stanford University Press, 1988). Steller wrote the journal, along with the zoological treatise 'De Bestiis Marinis', while shipwrecked and starving on Bering Island.

Glen Dye – *see NO 630 836.*

The Lily is a version of Il Giglio, by Donatella Bisutti, (Penetrali, Boetti & C. Editori 1989) translated by Pam Wardlaw.

The Garden – was it St Augustine who calculated Adam and Eve lasted only six hours in Paradise?

Calm Water at Mill Bay – after Bet Low 'Calm Water (At Mill Bay, Hoy)'.

Noust – A place of shelter, either natural or man made, where a boat may be hauled out in bad weather.